A Rose for Mat

A Narrative and Activity Book for Coping with Bereavement.

Nina Jackson, M.S.
Illustrated by D. Mannie

Acknowledgements

First, I would like to honor God for the insight to complete this project, and for giving me the strength to make this book available to those who are grieving. Secondly, I would like to say thank you to my family for helping me keep my dream alive. Last but not least, I would like to recognize the editors of this book. Without your eyes I would not have been able to keep the tone of this story authentic.

Copyright © 2004 by Nina Jackson. 543331
Library of Congress Control Number: 2003097766

ISBN: Softcover   978-1-4134-3245-9

Print information available on the last page.

Rev. date: 04/16/2019

To order additional copies of this book, contact:
Xlibris
1-888-795-4274
www.Xlibris.com
Orders@Xlibris.com

Table of Contents

Chapter 1: The Telephone Call

Everyone knew Grandma was in the hospital. Yet, they went on with their day as if everything was the same. After church, Dad went to the gym and Mom started Sunday dinner. To me this hospital stay for Grandma was different. There were many more telephone calls. Throughout the day, I sat around listening to every conversation Mom had with family members. I started to believe the things being said about Grandma "going away" and this was scary to me.

Less than ten minutes after Dad returned from the gym, the hospital called and said my parents should come as quickly as possible. I didn't want to go because I didn't want to see my Grandmother "go away". But, my parents didn't know how long they would be gone and there was no one to take care of me, so I went with them. "Besides all of your cousins will be there," Mom said.

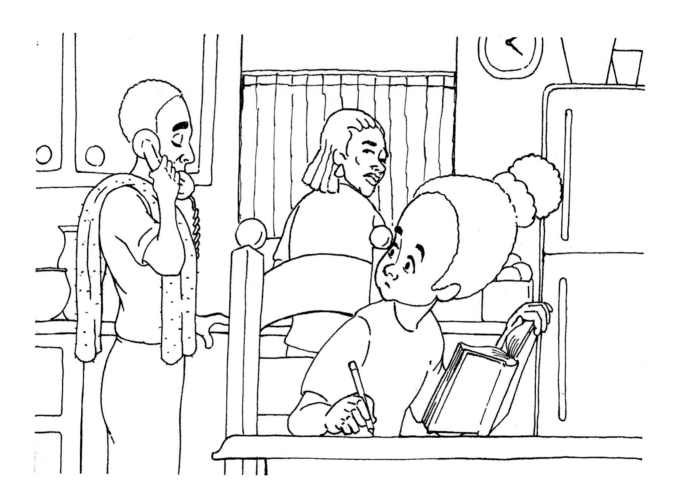

Chapter 2: The Ride to the Hospital

While riding in the car to the hospital no one said a word. A part of me wanted Dad to slow down. Just maybe it will happen while we are on our way, I thought. Another part of me wanted to be beamed right to the hospital. Just maybe if we are by her side, my best friend will not leave us, I thought.

Chapter 3: The Hospital Visit

When we arrived, all of the adults went into the closed-door area. The same area we left Grandma in the day before. I waited in the family area with my cousins Joey, Chris, and Imani.

Later, Uncle Joey, Sr. came out and requested we follow him into the room with the adults. I wasn't sure I wanted to know what was going on on the other side of the door, I went anyway. Once we entered the room everyone became silent. In the center of everyone was Grandma laying in a hospital bed. She looked like she was sleeping. But something about her was different. She was connected to machines with tubes and lots of lights. The strangest part about being in "the room" was I was no longer afraid and no one was crying. Everyone was telling Grandma how beautiful she looked and everything was going to be all right. "It's okay to go, Mama," Mom said. "You look like an angel just sleeping," said Aunt Jessica.

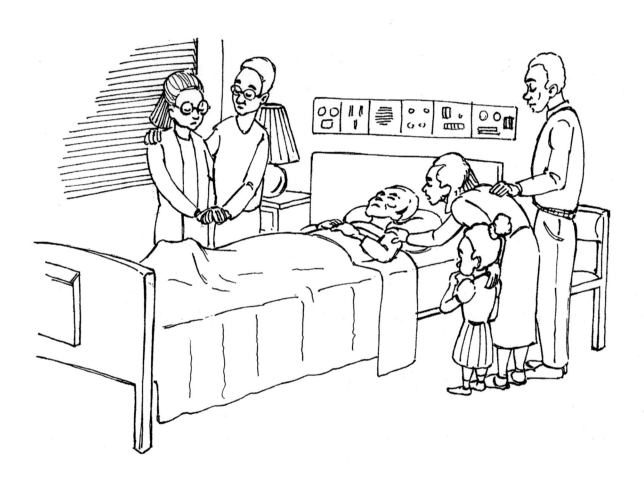

Then the doctor came in. He said the time, wrote it down, and we all kissed grandma good-bye. The adults went with the doctor and I went to the "cool" family room with my cousins.

Later I heard Cousin Mary say to Mom, "I will do anything you want me to do, but I am not planning to attend the **funeral**." "What's a funeral?" I asked. *"A funeral is a time to say good-bye and celebrate the life of the loved one who* **died** *(no longer living),"* Mom replied.

Chapter 4: The Day before the Funeral

It seemed like weeks had passed since I last saw Grandma. We lived so close to each other; I was use to seeing her everyday.

The day before the funeral was a lot of fun. I was with old friends, met new friends, and ate anything I wanted. The one person missing was Grandma and boy did I miss her. Some adults talked about seeing her. I asked Dad, "Is Grandma still at the hospital? How could people see her? Would you take me to see her?" He told me, "Those people saw Grandma at the **funeral home**. *A funeral home is a place where dead people are kept until their funeral.*"

He explained, "When we left the hospital, the **Funeral Director**, *the person in charge of the funeral home*, picked Grandma up in a **hearse** *(a special car that carries someone who has died)* and took her to the funeral home. At the funeral home, Grandma will be dressed and placed in a **casket** *(a box that dead people are placed in and buried)* for people to see her and say their good-byes." Dad also explained, "Your mother and I didn't think it was a good idea for you to see Grandma in a casket." Dad excused himself and came back with Mom.

Mom explained, "Tomorrow is the funeral. You don't have to go if you don't want to. During the funeral, Grandma will lay in the casket for us to see her. Some people will probably cry and that might make you sad. But, there will also be music, and people speaking about the things Grandma did in her life. This will also be the last time we'll see Grandma.

If you decide not to attend the funeral, Mrs. Persons will stay at Grandma's house with you. However, Dad and I will be attending the funeral. "

Dad explained, "After the funeral, Grandma will be placed in the hearse again and taken to her **grave** at the **cemetery**."What is a cemetery and a grave?" I asked. *"A cemetery is a place where dead people are* **buried**. *A grave is a hole either in the ground or in a building where dead people are* **buried**," Dad answered. "What's buried?" I asked. *"Buried is when the person who died is placed in the ground or in a building at the cemetery forever. After tomorrow the cemetery is where we'll go to take Grandma Flowers and to share stories with her,"* Mom answered.

Dad added, "We can share things with Grandma there. She won't talk back to us like she did when she was alive, she'll only talk to us in our hearts. You don't have to tell us right now if you are planning to attend the funeral, it's not until 10:00 a.m. tomorrow morning. If you decide not to go to the funeral, we'll find a special way for you to say good- bye to Grandma later."

Chapter 5: The Day of the Funeral

Dear God, today is the funeral and I think I would like to see Grandma one last time before my visits to the cemetery.

I walked into the kitchen and told my parents I wanted to see Grandma and I wanted to go to the funeral. "Good," Mom replied, "the **limousine** *(a large, fancy car)* will pick us up at Grandma's house in one hour."

When we got to Grandma's, there were three limousines there. I rode in the car with my cousins. Boy, it really felt special to ride in a limousine. It was large and all of us were able to fit into one car. This has never happened before.

When we arrived at the funeral home we walked in all together and there was Grandma dressed in her favorite blue dress, and laying in the casket. The chapel was full of family members, friends, and people I had never met before. We walked by the casket and I briefly looked at Grandma. People were right; she did look like she was sleeping. After we sat down, the pastor stood up and said nice things about my Grandma, Mattie. During the funeral there was singing, and crying. I cried so much I thought I would never stop. But I finally did. Every one cried and we all helped each other.

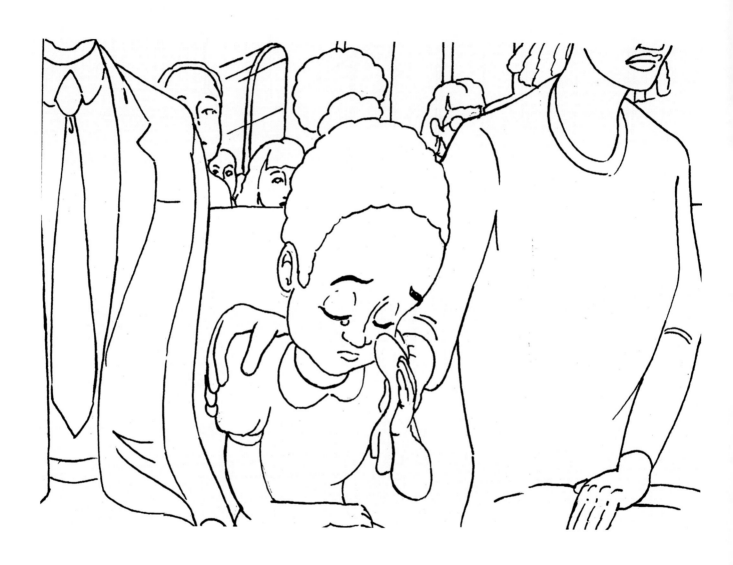

After the ceremony, the people in the audience walked by the casket to say their last good-byes. Then, it was the family's turn to say good-bye. I placed a pillow in the casket with Grandma. It was something I bought her one Mother's Day. I told her I wanted her to always have it with her. Once we all said our good-byes, the Funeral Director closed the casket and escorted Grandma to the hearse. We got back into our limousines and followed the hearse to the cemetery in a long line like a parade. The neat part of the parade line was the motorcycles that stopped traffic for us.

I thought a lot about Grandma during the ride to the cemetery. I thought about how special she was to me and how all those people who came to her funeral must have thought she was special too. I also thought to myself how Grandma was special enough to stop traffic and I smiled.

At the cemetery the pastor said a few words about Grandma, and people walked by and shook our hands. Then we left to go back to Grandma and Grandpa's house. It was nice to ride in a limousine, to stop traffic, and to see all those people that loved Grandma, but I still missed her.

Chapter 6: Grandma's House

After the guests left Grandma's house, I sat in her favorite chair and started to feel very sad. Dad walked over to me and said, "We can go to the cemetery anytime you want to visit Grandma. If you would like, we could even take her some roses from her rose garden." Grandpa whispered, "That would be nice. Mat always loved roses from her rose garden."

For a second, I felt better and I looked forward to taking roses to Grandma at the cemetery. I have a lot to share with her about the funeral, the motorcycles, and the limousine ride. I held my hand over my heart and said to myself, Grandma is there, even if it's only in my heart!

Chapter 7: Grief Drawings

Use these pages to draw how you felt before your loved one died, and how you felt after your loved one died.

This is how I felt before my loved one died.

Grief Drawings continued

This is how I felt after my loved one died.

Chapter 8: Journal Entries* *Small children may want to dictate their thoughts to an adult supporter to write as their journal entries.*

Use these pages to write to and about the person that died.

Today's Date: _____

Your Age: _____

Dear_____,

Today I am feeling

_____

_____

_____

_____

_____

_____

_____

_____

_____

_____

_____

_____

_____

_____

_____

_____

_____

_____

_____

_____

_____

Journal Entry

Today's Date: _____

Your Age: _____

Today I thought about _____ *and it made me*

_____

_____

_____

_____

_____

_____

_____

_____

_____

_____

_____

_____

_____

_____

_____

_____

_____

_____

_____

_____

_____

_____

Journal Entry

Today's Date: _____

Your Age: _____

I really miss _____

_____

_____

_____

_____

_____

_____

_____

_____

_____

A Rose for Mat

_____

_____

_____

_____

_____

_____

_____

_____

_____

_____

_____

_____

_____

Chapter 9: Dedication Page

Cut out and dedicate the heart and/or rose below to remember your loved one.

You are always in my heart.

A Rose For

Chapter 10: Bereavement Resources

The Compassionate Friends
P.O. Box 3696
Oak Brook, Illinois 60522-3696
U.S.A.
Telephone: (708) 990-0010
Fax: (708) 990-0246

Web address: www.compassionatefriends.org

The Compassionate Friends (TCF) is a national nonprofit, self-help support organization that offers friendship and understanding to bereaved parents, grandparents and siblings. There is no religious affiliation and there are no membership dues or fees. TCF offers national and local newsletters, books and tapes, and other related bereavement resources.

National Hospice Organization
1901 North Moore Street
Suite 901
Arlington, Virginia 22209
U.S.A.
Telephone: (800) 658-8898
Fax: (703) 525-5762

Web Address: www.nhpco.org

The only non-profit organization devoted entirely to promoting and maintaining quality hospice care for terminally ill persons and their families. NHO offers referrals to more than 2,100 hospices, a national newsletter, magazine, volunteer and professional conferences, and related support resources

Printed in the United States
By Bookmasters